WHEN DID COLUMBUS ARRIVE IN THE AMERICAS?

And Other Questions about Columbus's Voyages

Kathy Allen

LERNER PUBLICATIONS COMPANY · MINNEAPOLIS

A Word about Language

English word usage, spelling, grammar, and punctuation have changed over the centuries. Some spellings in this book have been changed from the original for better understanding.

Lerner Publications Company
A division of Lerner Publishing Group, Inc.
241 First Avenue North
Minneapolis, MN 55401 U.S.A.

Website address: www.lernerbooks.com

Library of Congress Cataloging-in-Publication Data

Allen, Kathy.
    When did Columbus arrive in the Americas? : and other questions about
  Columbus's voyages / by Kathy Allen.
        p.   cm. — (Six questions of American history)
    Includes bibliographical references and index.
    ISBN 978–0–7613–5327–0 (lib. bdg. : alk. paper)
    1. Columbus, Christopher—Juvenile literature. 2. America—Discovery and
  exploration—Juvenile literature. I. Title.
  E111.A38 2012
  970.01'5092—dc23   2011022550

Manufactured in the United States of America
1 – DP – 12/31/11

TABLE OF CONTENTS 4

THE SIX QUESTIONS HELP YOU DISCOVER THE FACTS!

INTRODUCTION

By October 1492, the crews of the *Niña*, the *Pinta*, and the *Santa Maria* were restless. The sailors had seen nothing but open ocean for two months. They had left the known world for riches and adventure in Asia. They had said good-bye to family and friends whom they might not see again. They worked and slept in driving rain and blazing sun. But was it all for nothing? Some had seen weeds in the water, a shorebird here and there—but no shining Asian cities.

Some in the crew were ready to rise up against their captain, Christopher Columbus. Some said Christopher Columbus was crazy. Others thought he was a master sailor with a fine sense of the sea. He had told the crew that they would reach the lands of China or Japan any day now. No one had ever traveled to Asia by sailing west from Europe. But Columbus promised that they would be the first.

Then, in the middle of the night on October 12, a man on the *Pinta* cried out "Land, land!" Moonlight sparkled in the waters ahead. The sailors raced to the deck to see what they could in the dark. Was this the golden land of riches they were searching for? Was their captain right after all? Who was this Christopher Columbus?

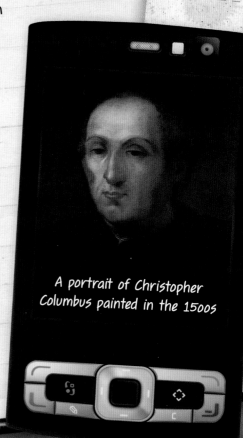

A portrait of Christopher Columbus painted in the 1500s

COLUMBUS'S FIRST VOYAGE

NORTH AMERICA

EUROPE

FRANCE

SPAIN

MARCH 3

Bayona

PORTUGAL

LISBON

Palos

S. LUCAR

CADIZ

PINTA

NIÑA

MARCH 15:
NIÑA AND PINTA
RETURN TO PALOS

FEBRUARY 13-14:
SHIPS SEPARATED
BY A STORM

AZORES

AUGUST 3, 1492:
COLUMBUS SAILS
FROM PALOS, SPAIN

OCTOBER 12, 1492:
COLUMBUS LANDS ON
SAN SALVADOR

BERMUDA

FEBRUARY 15:
NIÑA ARRIVES AT
SANTA MARIA ISLAND

OCTOBER
10

OCTOBER
7

CANARY
ISLANDS

SEPTEMBER
24

SEPTEMBER
16

SEPTEMBER
9

SEPTEMBER 30: SHIPS
COMPLETE 3 WEEKS WITH
NO SIGHT OF LAND

CUBA

HISPANIOLA

CARIBBEAN
SEA

SANTO
DOMINGO.

JANUARY 16, 1493:
NIÑA AND PINTA BEGIN
VOYAGE HOME

AUGUST 12: SHIPS
REACH GOMERA AND STAY
UNTIL SEPTEMBER 6

DECEMBER 25: SANTA
MARIA WRECKED

NORTH
ATLANTIC OCEAN

CAPE
VERDE

CENTRAL
AMERICA

AFRICA

N

EQUATOR

SOUTH AMERICA

SOUTH
ATLANTIC OCEAN

A Spanish artist of the late 1800s painted
this image of Columbus's ships, the *Pinta*,
the *Niña*, and the *Santa Maria*.

Genoa, Italy, was a thriving seaport during Columbus's time. This image was painted by Italian artist Cristoforo Grassi in the 1500s.

ONE BECOMING A CAPTAIN

Christopher Columbus was born near the sea in 1451. His family lived in Genoa, a city in what is modern-day Italy. Genoa was a trading center for countries bordering the Mediterranean Sea.

Columbus's parents were middle-class Christians. Columbus may have been tutored or sent to a monastery school. But his schooling was over by the time he turned fourteen.

He began working for Genoese merchants, whose ships traded throughout the Mediterranean area. In 1473 Columbus took part in a trip to Chios Island in the Aegean

people who buy and sell goods

6

Sea. The sea is between modern-day Greece and Turkey. This was the closest to Asia Columbus would ever get. Three years later, he nearly died in the Atlantic while sailing to northern Europe. French and Portuguese ships attacked the ships in his fleet. Columbus swam 6 miles (9.5 kilometers) back to land with the help of a floating oar.

a group of ships

In 1476 Columbus moved to Lisbon, Portugal. Portugal was a powerful country. It had some of the best sailing ships in the world. By the time Columbus moved there, he had started a career in sailing. He married Felipa Perestrello e Moniz, a noblewoman, in 1479. The following year, they had a son, Diego. To support his family, Columbus worked with his brother Bartholomew in a shop that made maps for sailors. Here, he learned more about geography and wind patterns.

a woman whose family is part of the ruling class

Columbus studied maps and wind patterns in order to know the best ways to sail the seas.

Living in Lisbon also gave Columbus sailing experiences. At least twice, he sailed southward to West Africa on trade missions. He traveled along an area the Portuguese called the Gold Coast (modern Ghana). It must have seemed like a new world to Columbus. The air was thick and warm and smelled of strange spices. The Portuguese even found gold there.

As Columbus learned about Africa and studied the sailing feats of the Portuguese, an idea formed in his mind. If sailors could reach this far south, might they be able to sail as far west across the Atlantic? Columbus was a skilled mapmaker, navigator, and sailor. Like most Europeans of his time, he knew the world was round. In the 1400s, many scholars believed that the world was fairly small and was covered mostly by land. Why had no one tried to cross the Atlantic Ocean? By sailing west, could one reach the East? Surely it could be done by the Portuguese navy, the best in the world.

Through friends, Columbus was able to ask King John II of Portugal for help to pay for such a voyage west.

navigator: a person who navigates, or guides, a sailing ship

HOW DID COLUMBUS GET HIS IDEA?

An early biography of Columbus explains why he thought sailing westward would bring him to Asia. "One thing leading to another and starting a train of thought, [Columbus], while in Portugal, began to speculate that if the Portuguese could sail so far south, it should be possible to sail as far westward, and that it was logical to expect to find land in that direction."

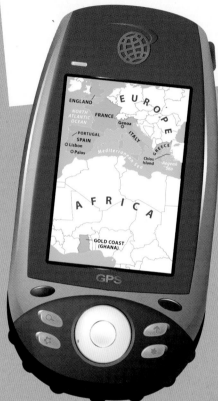

IMPORTANT PLACES
The places in green on this map are all places where Christopher Columbus lived or visited in his early life.

In 1485 the king turned him down. When Columbus's wife died later that year, he and his son moved to Spain, Portugal's neighbor to the east.

In his new country, Columbus met Beatriz Enríquez de Harana. They fell in love and had a son named Ferdinand a few years later. But Columbus wasn't giving up on finding a western route to Asia.

NEXT QUESTION

WHY DID COLUMBUS MOVE TO SPAIN?

This painting of King Ferdinand and Queen Isabella was made in the 1400s. Christopher Columbus asked the king and queen to help pay for his trip to Asia.

TWO A NOT-SO-SMALL WORLD

In Spain Columbus wrote letters asking to meet Ferdinand and Isabella, the Spanish king and queen. Meeting the king and the queen was no small wish. For a commoner, such a meeting was almost impossible. But Columbus had a powerful friend named Antonia de Marchena. She also wrote a letter recommending Columbus. Ferdinand and Isabella agreed to see Columbus. He thought the monarchs would like what he had to say.

At the time, there was no easy way to reach China. Christian Europeans were at war with the rulers of neighboring lands. European traders could not easily

commoner — a person who was not born into a royal or noble family

monarchs — kings, queens, or other rulers of a state or country

travel over land to the east. They risked being attacked or killed.

The Portuguese were trying to reach Asia by sailing around Africa. But Columbus thought he had a better, easier way. Sailing west, he said, would put Spain in direct contact with the Far East—China, Japan, and other parts of Southeast Asia. Europeans admired the civilization of China. Art, literature, and science thrived there. Europeans also saw China as a mysterious land of riches. Columbus claimed to be the best man to reach these lands. And he would do it by sea. The map he spread before the king and the queen in 1486 made the voyage look possible.

Columbus showed a map of his voyage to Ferdinand and Isabella.

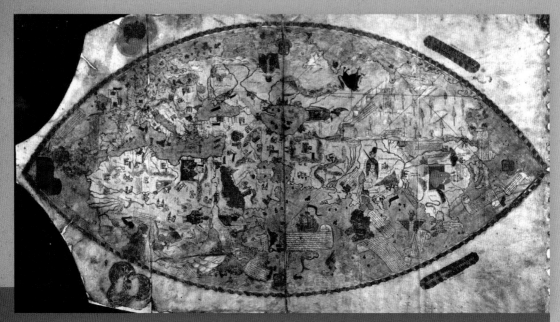

This map was drawn by Italian mathematician and astronomer Paolo Toscanelli (1397–1482) in 1474. The map led Columbus to believe he could sail westward to Asia.

Columbus thought he could reach China by sailing 5,000 miles (8,050 km) to the west. He also hoped to explore Japan, India, and a part of Southeast Asia that he called the West Indies. Ferdinand and Isabella gathered a panel of experts to look at Columbus's plan.

The experts did not believe that China, Japan, and India were so close. The panel thought the world was much bigger. Panel members also believed that the real distance to China was closer to 10,000 miles (16,100 km) and that the world was covered with more water than land. Ferdinand and Isabella trusted the experts and turned down Columbus's proposal.

WAS COLUMBUS THE FIRST TO CROSS THE ATLANTIC?

What Columbus didn't know is that sailors from Europe had already crossed the Atlantic. Nearly five hundred years before Columbus, Vikings had sailed from Greenland. They reached North America in what is modern-day Canada. Clothing, chess pieces, and other items have been found that prove the Vikings were in the New World before Columbus.

But Columbus tried to make his case to Spain's king and queen again a few years later. This time he claimed that he could spread Christianity to the lands he discovered. He also had some demands. He wanted to rule all lands he would discover on his journey. He wanted a noble title, Admiral of the Ocean Sea. And he wanted part of the riches he would bring back with him.

the leader of a navy

U.S. artist John Steeple Davis (1841–1917) created this image of Vikings landing in North America before Columbus's voyages.

This print from 1884 was made by Czechoslovakian artist Vaclav Brozik (1851–1901). It shows Columbus again asking the monarchs for money to explore a new route to the East.

He also asked that rule of the lands pass onto his sons, Diego and Ferdinand, upon his death. This common sailor was asking a lot. Again, the monarchs turned him down.

But his fortunes soon changed. In April 1492, King Ferdinand and Queen Isabella suddenly approved Columbus's plan. The agreements between Columbus and the monarchs were laid out in a paper called the Capitulations of Santa Fe. It stated: "Your Highnesses will also appoint the said Don

a term of honor

> "Your Highnesses grant to...
> Don Christopher one tenth of
> all merchandise, whether pearls,
> gems, gold, silver, spices, or
> goods of any kind."
> —Capitulations of santa Fe, 1492

Christopher their Viceroy and Governor-General in all islands and mainlands that, as has been stated, he may discover and acquire in the said Seas. . . . Your Highnesses grant to the said Don Christopher one tenth of all merchandise, whether pearls, gems, gold, silver, spices, or goods of any kind."

The monarchs changed their minds. The grand plan now had royal backing.

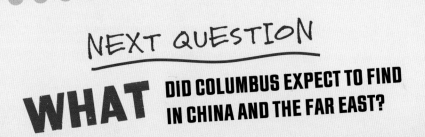

NEXT QUESTION

WHAT DID COLUMBUS EXPECT TO FIND IN CHINA AND THE FAR EAST?

These gold coins were found on a Spanish shipwreck from 1656. During Columbus's time and later, Spanish explorers sought to find gold for their country in their travels throughout the world.

THREE HIGH HOPES

King Ferdinand and Queen Isabella had changed their minds about Columbus's plan for many reasons. First and foremost, the purpose of Columbus's journey was to find a sea route to India, China, and Japan. Many kinds of goods could be found on such a route. At the top of the list was gold. The Asia of Europe's imagination had streets of gold. Columbus and his royal sponsors hoped he could find riches the likes of which Europe had never seen before.

persons or groups who agree to pay expenses or give support to other persons or groups

But gold was not all Columbus hoped to find. In the late 1400s, the diet of much of Europe was a bland mix of gruel, bread, and salted meat. The Spanish craved spices from the East—cinnamon, cloves, nutmeg, and sugar. These were new tastes in Europe. And these rare spices were costly. The hope of finding these and other goods, such as ivory and silk, in the Far East fueled the excitement around the preparation for this voyage.

a soft, chewy mixture of grain and water or milk

Ferdinand and Isabella were also sensitive to Spain's rivalry with Portugal. The two countries were fierce rivals in exploration and trade. A Portuguese explorer named Bartolomeu Dias had already found a route around the tip of Africa that led to the Indian Ocean. He could have continued to India and China. But his crew refused to go any farther. The men wanted to return to Portugal. The Spanish monarchs did not want to lose the race to Asia.

Cinnamon and nutmeg were among the spices that were traded in the East. Columbus sailed west in an effort to reach the spice lands of Asia.

THE CATHOLIC MONARCHS

One of the main reasons Queen Isabella approved Columbus's journey was her interest in spreading the Christian faith. Christians at the time held a great fear that Islam—another faith practiced in the Mediterranean area—would spread across Europe. Queen Isabella and King Ferdinand were known as the Catholic Monarchs.

In addition, a greater concern weighed on Columbus and the royal family. King Ferdinand and Queen Isabella were extremely religious. Columbus knew they would be interested in spreading Christianity. He wrote in a 1492 letter to Ferdinand and Isabella:

> *Your Highnesses, as Catholic Christians and Princes, lovers and promoters of the Holy Christian Faith . . . you thought of sending me . . . to the said regions of India to see the said princes and to see how their conversion to our Holy Faith might be undertaken.*

By claiming lands along Columbus's route, the Spanish monarchs hoped to establish Christianity in more of the world.

Columbus believed that God would guide his ships. But Columbus was not sailing only as a servant of God. He wanted to raise his fortune and his standing in society.

Ferdinand and Isabella's support helped Columbus get three ships and a crew to work on them. As the fleet prepared

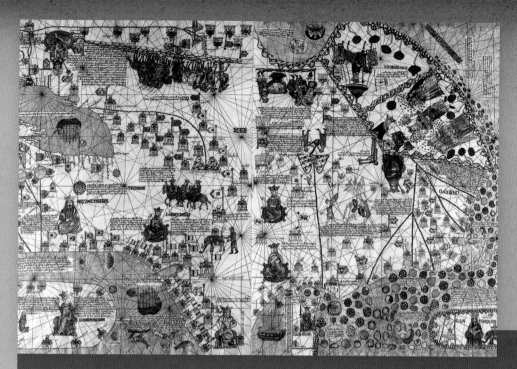

Mapmaker Cresques Abraham illustrated the Catalan Atlas in 1375. He included information about cities, such as their political and religious connections. Ferdinand and Isabella, hoping to spread Christianity to other lands, decided to fund Columbus's voyage.

to sail from Palos, Spain, the air was alive with energy. Columbus and his crew were ready for adventure. While they hoped to find riches, they couldn't be sure they would. The lure of the unknown propelled them as the three ships left harbor on August 3, 1492.

NEXT QUESTION

HOW DID COLUMBUS NAVIGATE HIS ROUTE?

Christopher Columbus bids farewell to Queen Isabella as he and his crew depart from Spain in August 1492. This print was made in 1893.

FOUR DEAD RECKONING

The ships that Columbus led that day were the best in the world for their mission. Columbus wanted smaller ships that could sail in shallow water, making them safer for exploring new coasts. The *Niña* and the *Pinta* were small, light, speedy caravels. The *Niña* could carry about 52 tons (47 metric tons), including cargo—firewood, food, and sailing supplies such as canvas and rope. The *Pinta* could carry about 60 tons (54 metric tons). Columbus sailed on the larger, slower *Santa Maria*. The *Santa Maria* was a *nao*, which is larger and rounder than a caravel. We cannot know just how large each ship was, but caravels were

sailing vessels that can carry about 60 tons (54 metric tons)

SQUARE-RIGGED SHIPS

The ships in Columbus's fleet were square-rigged for sailing across the open ocean. Square-rigged sails are attached to a spar (a rounded piece of wood) that is horizontal, or square, to the hull of the ship. A triangular sail, known as a lateen, runs at an angle from the back to the front of the boat. Light, lateen-rigged ships were good for sailing into the wind and for easier maneuvering.

generally 70 to 80 feet (21 to 24 meters) long. All the ships were made of wood.

Each ship was rigged differently for different sailing conditions. Square-rigged ships were good for sailing across open water when the wind was at their backs. At times, the *Niña* was fitted with lateen (triangular) rigging, which made it easier to move among the islands or into an inlet, for example.

a bay or a narrow water passage

Two of Columbus's ships—the *Niña* and the *Pinta*—were typical Spanish caravels. The *Santa Maria (center)* was larger and carried more supplies.

Columbus and his crew had to live aboard their ships for months. At one point, as hopes of sighting land grew dim, the crew wanted to overthrow their captain.

Each ship had a crew of sailors, officers, and a captain. Columbus was the captain of the *Santa Maria*. Two brothers were the captains of the *Pinta* and the *Niña*. But Columbus struggled to find men for the crews. The monarchs even pardoned any criminal willing to serve on the crews. The *Niña* and the *Pinta* probably had about twenty men. The *Santa Maria* probably carried about twice that many.

All the ships were open. The men on deck were not sheltered from wind and rain. Any covered space below the deck would have been used for cargo. Each man had only a small chest on board with him. He changed between two sets of clothes for the entire trip. He bathed in the ocean, and his beard grew longer every day. There were no bathrooms, so the men leaned over the side of the ship. They slept on deck and used a rope as a pillow. They ate in the same crowded, dirty space where they worked and slept.

Columbus had told the crew that the trip would take about three weeks. But three weeks passed, and still no land was in sight. The crew had good reason to believe in Columbus's skills. He had mastered a navigation method called dead reckoning. It provided a crude way to measure longitude. Dead reckoning uses speed and direction to give a rough guess about where a ship is. Columbus measured speed by throwing a log or a float in the water. The log was attached to a rope. Columbus could see how long it took the log to pass by the ship. He used an hourglass to measure time and a quadrant to measure direction.

the position of a place, measured in degrees east or west of a line that runs north and south through Greenwich, England

an instrument used to measure angles

This quadrant is from 1760. Quadrants helped sailors navigate on the seas by using the position of certain stars.

the star in the Northern Hemisphere toward which the axis of Earth points

the distance north or south from the equator, measured from 0 to 90 degrees

He used the quadrant to measure the position of the North Star. Tracing a line from the star to the horizon, Columbus could determine which way was north. The angle of the star on the horizon would give Columbus his latitude. For example, if the quadrant showed that the North Star was on the horizon at a 25° angle, the ship would be at 25° north. When south of the equator, though, the North Star is not visible, so Columbus would have used the sun. Either way, dead reckoning was a crude system that Columbus used very well.

As the weeks passed, however, the crew began to doubt Columbus. They had been at sea for two months and one

Columbus and his crew finally spotted land after more than two months at sea. Did Columbus find a route to Asia as he had set out to do?

week, much longer than Columbus had expected. Some men threatened to rise up against him. But Columbus convinced them to sail for just three more days. The next day, the crew saw weeds in the water below them and shorebirds above them. Hopes were rising. Then, in the middle of the night on October 12, a sailor on the *Pinta* spotted land. Shouts of "Tierra! [Land]" rang out across the ships.

NEXT QUESTION

WHERE HAD COLUMBUS LANDED?

Columbus and his men met Native Americans upon landing in San Salvador. The native peoples, known as Tainos, looked and acted very differently from Europeans.

FIVE THE VOYAGES

At first light, Columbus anchored his ships. Then the crew set out for land in small boats. The shore they had come to was probably an island in the Caribbean Sea. Columbus named it San Salvador. This was not a new world in the sense that no one had been there before. The Taino people already lived there. Columbus and his crew traded glass beads and other small items with them.

The Taino were part of a larger group of people called the Arawaks. But Columbus thought he was in the East Indies, near China or India, so he called them Indians. The Arawaks guided Columbus as he sailed from island to

THE ARAWAKS

The Arawaks were a group of native peoples who settled in South America and across the Caribbean. The Arawaks that Columbus met wore little clothing. They wore gold nose rings and necklaces. They sometimes painted their bodies with dyes. Columbus described them in a letter announcing his discovery:

All that I saw were young men, none of them more than 30 years old, very well made, of very handsome bodies and very good faces; the hair coarse and almost as the hair of a horse's tail and short.... They bear no arms, nor know thereof; for I showed them swords and they grasped them by the blade and cut themselves through ignorance.

European explorers were very interested in the peoples they met. French artist Charles Plumier painted this image of a Caribbean native holding weapons for a book published in 1686.

island. He was looking for the riches of the Asian mainland. He marveled at the plants and fish that no one in the crew had ever seen before.

As the sun set on Saturday, October 27, they approached the island of modern-day Cuba. Columbus thought it must be Japan. But as he explored the shores, he decided that it was not an island. This must be China, he thought. This must be the Asian mainland. But if it was China, where were the golden cities?

Columbus lands on the island of Hispaniola. In this 1728 illustration by a Spanish artist, the local Arawaks bring gold and treasures to Columbus and his crew.

Columbus sailed south until he came to what is modern-day Haiti and the Dominican Republic. He named the island Hispaniola, because it reminded him of Spain (Hispania Hispania was an old name for Spain). On Hispaniola, Columbus finally found signs of gold. The Arawaks here traded gold and told him of more gold elsewhere on the island. Columbus took what gold he could to avoid returning to Spain empty-handed. He was also set on taking some Arawaks to Spain.

By late 1492, Columbus's crew had had its first battle with the native peoples. Then the *Santa Maria* ran aground on Christmas Eve. Columbus decided to return to Spain with

run onto the shore

the two remaining ships. He left about forty of his men on Hispaniola and promised he would return.

The journey home was stormy and difficult, but Columbus made it back to Spain. He brought exotic parrots, what gold pieces he had, and the few Arawaks who had survived the trip. His finds caused quite a stir. Columbus began to prepare for a second trip right away.

unfamiliar or from another land

Isabella and Ferdinand welcome Columbus back to Spain. He brought with him native Arawaks, exotic fruits, and riches he discovered on his voyage. French artist Eugène Devéria (1808–1865) painted this image of Columbus's homecoming.

This time, the monarchs told him to expand the Hispaniola colony, convert the natives to Christianity, and find more gold. And there was no need to pardon criminals for the next crew. This time Columbus had many volunteers, including his brothers, Diego and Bartholomew. Columbus led a fleet of seventeen ships from a festive going-away party at the harbor. The fleet left from Cadiz, Spain, on September 25, 1493.

Again using dead reckoning, Columbus made landfall in just three weeks on a Caribbean island he named Dominica. But his good spirits sank when he went back to Hispaniola.

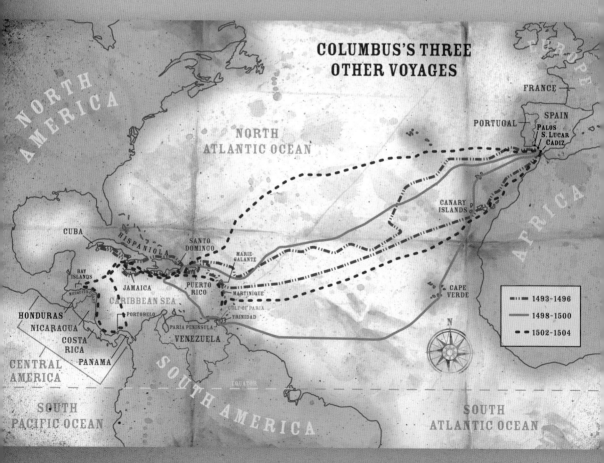

COLUMBUS'S THREE OTHER VOYAGES

NORTH AMERICA

EUROPE

NORTH ATLANTIC OCEAN

FRANCE

PORTUGAL

SPAIN
PALOS
S. LUCAR
CADIZ

CANARY ISLANDS

AFRICA

CUBA

HISPANIOLA

SANTO DOMINGO

MARIE-GALANTE

BAY ISLANDS

JAMAICA

PUERTO RICO

MARTINIQUE

CAPE VERDE

MOSQUITO

CARIBBEAN SEA

GULF OF PARIA

HONDURAS

PORTOBELO

TRINIDAD

NICARAGUA

PARIA PENINSULA

COSTA RICA

VENEZUELA

CENTRAL AMERICA

PANAMA

N

| ----- 1493-1496 |
| ——— 1498-1500 |
| - - - 1502-1504 |

SOUTH PACIFIC OCEAN

EQUATOR

SOUTH AMERICA

SOUTH ATLANTIC OCEAN

The Spaniards forced the Arawaks to search for gold.

The men he had left there were gone. They had been killed in fights with the Arawaks and with one another. Columbus set up another colony, called Isabella, and put his brothers in charge. He sent several ships back to Spain for more supplies.

Meanwhile, Columbus explored Cuba. The land was so large that Columbus was convinced the island was actually the Asian mainland. But he found little gold there and returned to Hispaniola.

The colony on Hispaniola was falling apart. Columbus and his men had not found the gold they hoped to bring back to Spain. They enslaved the natives and made them work to find more. Some of the men who had returned to Spain for supplies told the king and the queen that the colony was failing under the poor leadership of Columbus. In March 1496, Columbus decided to return home.

Columbus's coat of arms represented his status and occupation. It displayed a castle (upper left), a lion (upper right), islands in a wavy sea (bottom left), and anchors (lower right).

The trip home was slow, and the men nearly ran out of food and supplies. Columbus did not reach Spain until June. There, he persuaded the monarchs to fund a third journey. He told them he could find the riches of the East and claim the land for Spain. But this time, Ferdinand and Isabella were more careful.

For his third voyage, Columbus had only six ships in his fleet. He left from Sanlúcar, Spain, on May 30, 1498. He had orders to explore south of where he had already been. On July 31, Columbus landed in the Gulf of Paria off the island of Trinidad. When he crossed the gulf, he could hardly believe his eyes. Freshwater streamed into the gulf before him. This was no island. Columbus had reached the mainland, but it was not the mainland of China. He was off the coast of modern-day Venezuela in South America. He thought this new land was a kind of heaven on earth. He believed he had found the Garden of Eden.

But he wouldn't be in paradise for long. In August Columbus returned to Hispaniola to find that the plan to colonize Hispaniola was not going well. Colonists returning to Spain had complained about mistreatment of the Tainos. They also complained about Columbus misgoverning the colony.

In the summer of 1498, Columbus landed on the shore of what would become Venezuela.

Ferdinand and Isabella sent an investigator named Francisco de Bobadilla there to see if the claims against Columbus were true. Bobadilla found sickness and the start of revolts in the island colony. The investigator claimed that Columbus and his brothers were failing to manage the colony. A colony such as this, Bobadilla thought, would never survive. Columbus had failed to do what he had promised. He was failing at claiming the lands he found for Spain. Bobadilla put Columbus and his brothers under arrest and sent them back to Spain in chains.

Columbus returns to Spain for a third time—this time in chains. In August 1498, court investigator Francisco de Bobadilla sought the truth to the claims that Columbus mismanaged the colonization of Hispaniola. He had Columbus arrested.

The monarchs let Columbus keep his titles, but he could no longer govern Hispaniola. The king and queen appointed Nicholás de Ovando to serve as governor. They sent him to the island with thirty ships and about twenty-five hundred colonists.

Columbus was losing the race to find a passage to Asia. Ferdinand and Isabella were losing patience with him. They were hesitant about giving Columbus yet another chance. The king and queen had heard that Portuguese explorer Vasco da Gama had already reached India by sailing around Africa. But Columbus tried to convince them that he was close to achieving his goal. In the end, Ferdinand and Isabella agreed to give Columbus one last chance to find his passage.

Columbus called this fourth trip the High Voyage. Columbus thought that on this voyage he would finally discover the riches of the Far East. Columbus sailed from Cadiz with four ships in May 1502. By his side was his fourteen-year-old son, Ferdinand.

Smooth sailing took the fleet to the Caribbean island of Martinique on June 15. Columbus tried to go to Hispaniola, but the new governor turned him away. By the end of July, Columbus had reached what later came to be called Central America. For almost one year, he and his fleet sailed along the shores of modern-day Honduras, Nicaragua, Costa Rica, and Panama, searching for a passage to Asia. During a storm, strong winds and rain damaged the ships. The crew ran them ashore on the island of Jamaica. They were marooned there for a year. One of Columbus's sailors managed to canoe to Hispaniola for help. Seven months later, Ovando sent a ship to rescue them and send them back to Spain.

put ashore on an island and unable to get back to sea

NEXT QUESTION

WHEN DID COLUMBUS BECOME FAMOUS?

SIX A CHANGED WORLD

Columbus died on May 20, 1506, within two years after returning to Spain. He did not have the respect and standing that he had hoped for. He believed that he had found the Asian mainland. But he was one of the few people to think so. Shortly after his death, Columbus's bones were moved to Hispaniola and Cuba. They were sent back to Spain in 1795.

For almost three hundred years, most people didn't know who Christopher Columbus was. When the people close to him died, so did the memory of him. But Columbus's son Ferdinand wrote a biography of his father.

A scientist points to a box that is believed to contain the remains of Christopher Columbus. Some experts believe that Columbus's health may have been failing as early as his third trip. At that time, he had been suffering from poor eyesight, fatigue, and joint problems.

It wasn't published until 1571. It was translated into English in 1744.

In the United States, Columbus gained recognition after the Revolutionary War (1775–1783). After the colonies broke away from Britain, people wanted a hero who was not British. They made the man who braved the unkown into that hero. Colonists found inspiration in his courage and spirit. Ferdinand's biography of his father became popular. Ferdinand had idolized his father. So did the newly independent citizens of the United States. They began naming things after him, including the *Columbus*, a warship in the Continental navy in 1775. As the new nation became great, so did the memory of its hero.

The world's view of Columbus has changed over time. Many people have become critical of the effect Columbus's voyages had on the native Tainos and Arawaks. Fifty years after first coming into contact with Columbus and Spanish colonists, almost all the Arawaks were dead. Many died from working in fields and gold mines for the European colonists. Forced labor began under the rule of Columbus's brothers in Hispaniola. Natives who did not collect enough gold were punished or killed.

Queen Isabella wanted the Arawaks to be converted, not enslaved. But if they refused to convert, slavery was their fate. In trying to convert the natives, Columbus was almost ensuring that they would be enslaved.

Those natives who did not die from overwork died of starvation or disease. The Spanish introduced diseases such as smallpox, diphtheria, measles, and whooping cough. The Arawaks had never been exposed to such diseases. They were not immune to them. Entire families became sick at the same time.

immune: protected from a disease

Other things the Europeans introduced were helpful. They brought animals such as cattle, goats, horses, pigs, and sheep to the New World. In modern times, it would be hard to imagine the Americas without these animals. Europeans also introduced crops such as wheat, yams, and bananas. In turn, Europeans found corn and potatoes in the Americas. Such foods soon became a big part of the European diet.

Americas: North America, South America, and Central America collectively

NAMED FOR COLUMBUS

One way Columbus's legacy can be seen is in all the places and things named after him, including the following:

- Columbia University
- Columbus, Ohio
- Colombia (a country in South America)
- Washington, D.C. (District of Columbia)
- The space shuttle *Columbia*

The exchange of people from the Old World to the New World had a huge impact. Most people who live in the Americas speak languages from Europe such as English and Spanish. Many of the religions and governments of the Americas are also much like those found in Europe. Columbus joined the two worlds together, for good or bad. His legacy is debated, but most people agree that his voyages to the Americas changed the world forever.

> legacy — something that comes from the past

NEXT QUESTION

HOW DO WE KNOW ABOUT THE VOYAGES OF COLUMBUS?

Primary Source: Columbus's Diary

The best way to learn about any historical event is with primary sources. A primary source is something produced by someone living at the time an event happened. Primary sources include diaries, newspaper articles, pamphlets, letters, documents, speeches, photos, and other items.

Columbus wrote at least two letters to King Ferdinand and Queen Isabella. He described what he saw in the New World. His son Ferdinand also wrote a biography of his father. But the best source is Columbus himself, writing in his journal, or diary. A copy of a copy of the original has survived into modern times. It describes his first trip in 1492:

> I determined to keep an account of the voyage, and to write down punctually every thing we performed or saw from day to day, as will hereafter appear.
>
> Saturday, 13 October [the day after sighting land]:
> At daybreak great multitudes of men came to the shore, all young and of fine shapes, very handsome; their hair not curled but straight and coarse . . . their eyes were large and very beautiful. . . . This is a large and level island, with trees extremely flourishing, and streams of water; there is a large lake in the middle of the island, but no mountains: the whole is completely covered with verdure [plants] and delightful to behold.

TELL YOUR COLUMBUS STORY

You are an officer aboard the *Santa Maria* on Columbus's first journey across the Atlantic. Write a letter to your family back home telling them what you've seen and done and what you hope to discover.

WHO are you, and to whom are you writing?

WHAT do you think of your captain, Christopher Columbus?

WHEN do you think you'll reach land?

WHERE do you think you'll land?

WHY did you decide to be part of the crew on such a risky voyage?

WHAT is daily life like on a ship?

HOW do you plan to pass the time on the long trip?

USE **WHO, WHAT, WHERE, WHY, WHEN,** AND **HOW** TO THINK OF OTHER QUESTIONS TO HELP YOU CREATE YOUR STORY!

Timeline

1451
Christopher Columbus is born to a middle-class family in Genoa, Italy.

1479
Columbus marries Felipa Perestrello e Moniz.

1480
Columbus's son Diego is born.

1485
King John II of Portugal refuses to fund Columbus's trans-Atlantic voyage.
Columbus's wife, Felipa, dies.

1486
King Ferdinand and Queen Isabella reject the chance to fund a trans-Atlantic voyage to Asia.

1488
Columbus's son Ferdinand is born.

1492
Columbus finally wins royal approval for his voyage. The *Niña*, the *Pinta*, and the *Santa Maria* sail from Palos, Spain, on August 3.

On October 12, a sailor on the *Pinta* spots land. The fleet lands at San Salvador.

On October 28, Columbus lands in Cuba, which he thinks is China. Columbus later sails to Hispaniola, where he finds gold.

1493
Columbus returns to Spain. He leaves thirty-nine men on Hispaniola.

Columbus's second journey begins. He leads seventeen ships from Cadiz, Spain, on September 25.

Columbus reaches Hispaniola on November 23. The men he left are nowhere to be found. He leaves to explore Cuba.

1496

Crew members complain about poor leadership by Columbus and his brothers. Columbus returns to Spain to defend himself to the king and the queen.

1498

Ferdinand and Isabella grant Columbus a fleet of six ships for a journey that departs from Sanlúcar, Spain, on May 30.

On July 31, Columbus observes freshwater off the coast of Venezuela. He knows he has discovered a new continent and believes it must be Asia.

1500

A Spanish investigator finds the colony of Hispaniola in revolt. **Columbus is arrested** and sent back to Spain in chains.

1502

The monarchs free Columbus and grant him one final chance to find a sea route to Asia. He commands a fleet of four ships that sails from Cadiz, Spain, on May 9.

In July the fleet arrives in modern-day Honduras and travels south.

1503

The last two ships in Columbus's fleet are grounded off modern-day Jamaica. One year later, the shipwrecked crew is rescued. Columbus returns to Spain for the final time.

1506

Columbus dies on May 20 in Valladolid, Spain.

1571

Ferdinand's biography of his father is published.

1744

Ferdinand's biography is translated into English.

Source Notes

8 Zvi Dor-Ner, *Columbus and the Age of Discovery* (New York: HarperCollins, 1992), 76.

14–15 Ibid., 104.

15 Ibid.

18 Margarita Zamora, *Reading Columbus* (Berkeley: University of California Press, 1993), 29.

24 Samuel Morison, *Admiral of the Ocean Sea—A Life of Christopher Columbus* (New York: Little, Brown, 1942), 230, available online at http://books.google .com/books?id=T5x5xjsJtIwC&printsec=frontcover&dq=admiral+of+the+ocean+s ea&hl=en&ei=JybfTJ3pCMzvngf35LHqDw&sa=X&oi=book_result&ct=result&res num=1&ved=0CDAQ6AEwAA#v=onepage&q&f=false (November 3, 2011).

42 Paul Halsall Mar, ed., "Medieval Sourcebook: Christopher Columbus: Extracts from Journal," Fordham University, http://www.fordham.edu/halsall/source/ columbus1.asp (September 1, 2011).

Selected Bibliography

Dor-Ner, Zvi. *Columbus and the Age of Discovery*. New York: HarperCollins, 1992.

Feegan, William. *Sailing into History*. 1991. http://www.flmnh.ufl.edu/ caribarch/columbus.htm#rumbo (November 3, 2011).

Mar, Paul Halsall, ed. "Medieval Sourcebook: Christopher Columbus: Extracts from Journal." 1996. http://www.fordham.edu/halsall/source/columbus1.html (November 3, 2011).

Morison, Samuel. *Admiral of the Ocean Sea—A Life of Christopher Columbus*. New York: Little, Brown, 1942. Available online at http://books.google.com/ books?id=T5x5xjsJtIwC&printsec=frontcover&dq=admiral+of+the+ocean+sea&h l=en&ei=JybfTJ3pCMzvngf35LHqDw&sa=X&oi=book_result&ct=result&resnum =1&ved=0CDAQ6AEwAA#v=onepage&q&f=false (November 3, 2011).

Newton, Arthur. *The Great Age of Discovery*. New York: Lenox Hill, 1932. Available online at http://books.google.com/books?id=qmvru6Xwu-IC&printsec= frontcover#v=onepage&q&f=false (November 3, 2011).

Office of Naval Research. "Science and Technology Focus: Observing the Sky." ONR. N.d. http://www.onr.navy.mil/focus/spacesciences/observingsky/ constellations4.htm (November 3, 2011).

Tirado, Thomas C. "Christopher Columbus." *Encarta*. N.d. Available online at: http://phobos.ramapo.edu/~rchristo/christopher_columbus.htm (November 3, 2011).

Smithsonian. "Vikings: The North Atlantic Saga." MNH. http://www.mnh.si.edu/vikings/start.html (November 3, 2011).

Zamora, Margarita. *Reading Columbus*. Berkeley: University of California Press, 1993.

Further Reading and Websites

Aller, Susan Bivin. *Christopher Columbus*. Minneapolis: Lerner Publications Company, 2003. This attractive biography is illustrated with historical photographs and artwork.

Christopher Columbus
http://www.flmnh.ufl.edu/caribarch/columbus.htm
This comprehensive look at Columbus in the Americas includes a list of crew members on each ship.

Mann, Charles. *Before Columbus: The Americas of 1491*. New York: Atheneum, 2009. Mann explores the Americas pre-Columbus with illustrations and photos.

Markle, Sandra. *Animals Christopher Columbus Saw*. San Francisco: Chronicle, 2008. Markle uses Columbus's log to describe animals in the New World.

Wulffson, Don. *Before Columbus*. Minneapolis: Twenty-First Century Books, 2007. This book discusses other groups who may have come to the Americas before Columbus and even before the Vikings.

Index

Photo Acknowledgments

The images in this book are used with the permission of: © iStockphoto.com/DNY59, p. 1; © Tamara Bauer/ Dreamstime.com, pp. 1 (background) and all wave pattern backgrounds; © iStockphoto.com/sx70, pp. 3 (top), 8, 13 (top), 18, 21 (top), 27 (left), 41 (top); © iStockphoto.com/Ayse Nazli Deliormanli, pp. 3 (bottom), 43 (bottom left); © iStockphoto.com/Serdar Yagci, pp. 4–5; © iStockphoto.com/Andrey Pustovoy (smart phone), pp. 4, 17, 23, 32, 39; © Giraudon/The Bridgeman Art Library, p. 4 (inset), 29; © Laura Westlund/ Independent Picture Service (maps), pp. 4-5, 9, 30; © Index/The Bridgeman Art Library, p. 5 (bottom); Naval Museum Genoa/Collection Dagli Orti/The Art Archive/Art Resource, NY., p. 6; © North Wind Picture Archives, pp. 7, 31; © iStockphoto.com/Talshiar, p. 9 (GPS); © Convento Agustinas, Madrigal, Avila/The Bridgeman Art Library, p. 10; © North Wind Picture Archives/Alamy, pp. 11, 21 (bottom), 24, 34; The Granger Collection, New York, pp. 12, 13 (bottom), 28, 45; © Archive Images/Alamy, pp. 14, 20; © Jeffrey Rotman/CORBIS, p. 16; © Paul Poplis/Foodpix/Getty Images, p. 17 (inset); © J. Bedmar/Iberfoto/The Image Works, p. 19 (top); © Peter Newark Historical Pictures/The Bridgeman Art Library, pp. 22, 26; © Adams George/The Bridgeman Art Library, p. 23 (inset); © Archives Charmet/The Bridgeman Art Library, p. 27 (right); Museo Navale Pegli/ Gianni Dagli Orti/The Art Archive/Art Resource, NY., p. 32 (inset); © Angel Rodriguez/Photodisc/Getty Images, p. 33; © National Museum of Ancient Art, Libson, Portugal/The Bridgeman Art Library, p. 35; © Biblioteca Colombina, Seville, Spain/The Bridgeman Art Library, p. 36; Seville Cathedral/Gianni Dagli Orti/ The Art Archive/Art Resource, NY., p. 38; © Reuters/CORBIS, p. 39 (inset); © Dorling Kindersley/Getty Images, p. 43 (bottom right); © Museu de Marinha/The Bridgeman Art Library, p. 44.

Front cover: © English School/The Bridgeman Art Library/Getty Images. Back cover: © Tamara Bauer/ Dreamstime.com (background).

Main body text set in Sassoon Sans Regular 13.5/20. Typeface provided by Monotype Typography.